RESISTANCE

Victor Serge

Translated from the French by James Brook

City Lights Books
San Francisco

Library of Congress Cataloging-in-Publication Data

Serge, Victor, 1890-1947.
  [Résistance. English]
  Resistance : selected poems / by Victor Serge; translated by James Brook.
    p. cm.
  Translation of Résistance.
  ISBN: 0-87286-225-9 : $5.95
    1. Serge, Victor. 1890-1947—Translations, English.
2. Revolutionary poetry, French —.Translations into English.
3. Revolutionary poetry. English —.Translations from French.
I. Title.
PQ2637.E49A23   1989
841'.912.—.dc19   88-16869

City Lights Books are available to bookstores through our primary distributor: Subterranean Company, P.O. Box 10233, Eugene OR 97440. 1-800-274-7826.
Our books are also available through library jobbers and regional distributors. For personal orders and catalogs, please write to City Lights Mail Order: 261 Columbus Avenue, San Francisco CA 94133.

CITY LIGHTS BOOKS are edited by Lawrence Ferlinghetti and Nancy J. Peters and published at the City Lights Bookstore, 261 Columbus Avenue, San Francisco.

TRANSLATOR'S NOTE

Every literary work is the product of collaboration, and this translation is no exception. Richard Greeman, Donald Nicholson-Smith, Ken Knabb, and, at City Lights, Lawrence Ferlinghetti, Nancy Peters, and Philip Lamantia gave the manuscript a careful reading and greatly improved it with their corrections and suggestions. An ever enthusiastic supporter of this project, Richard Greeman also enlisted Vlady in our efforts to resolve ambiguities in his father's poems. I can only acknowledge my debt to my collaborators; I can never discharge it.

—J.B.

To my companions in captivity in 1933-1936,
Boris Yeltsin, Pevzner, Chernykh, Bielenkii, Byk, Lakhovitski,
Santalov, Lyda Svalova, Fayna Upstein, left communists,

Nesterov and Yegoritch, right communists,

without knowing whether they are dead or alive,

but with the certainty that whether dead or live, resisters or torture
victims, these men and women remain, in the shipwrecked
revolution, an example of total and lucid fidelity to the true
revolution.

Note

With the exception of four pieces in the same spirit that were written in
Petrograd in 1920-28 and recently in Paris, I have collected here the poems
I wrote in Russia in 1935-36 during the period of deportation that I spent in
Orenburg: I had to recompose them later, since the Soviet censor did not
allow me to take any of my manuscripts with me.

Another will tear up the prison records.
Another will break down the doors of the jail.
Another will wipe from our thin shoulders
The dust and blood fallen from our necks.

—Péguy

CONTENTS

Richard Greeman is the translator of four of Victor Serge novels: *Men in Prison, Birth of Our Power, Conquered City,* and *Midnight in the Century* (Writers & Readers Publishing Cooperative, N.Y. and London). He is currently completing a book on Serge's life and works for publication during the Serge Centennial Year, 1990.

INTRODUCTION

by Richard Greeman

Victor Serge (1890-1947) is best known as a revolutionary and a novelist, but his need to people his inner solitudes with poetic presences was permanent, so that poetry occupied an important place throughout his tumultuous life. Among his earliest writings we find a poem, *"Que deviendrons-nous, ô destin sournois!"* (Paris, 1912), which already exhibits a mature command of language. He is writing poetry in the middle of the Russian Civil War — "City" (Petrograd, 1920) — and the bulk of the poems presented here date from his years of semi-captivity in Central Asia (1933-35). There are poems composed during the fall of France — "The Rats Flee" (1941), and the last text Serge completed before his death was the magnificent elegy, "Hands" (Mexico, 1947) with its intimations of mortality and its profound sense of fraternal communion across the ages — through suffering, through consciousness, through art.

Indeed, his novels themselves are strewn with snatches of verse and passages of such density and evocative power as to merit the designation of prose-poems. It is thus with gratitude and a sense of appropriateness that we welcome this collection of Serge's poetry in James Brook's faithful translation on the eve of Serge's Centenary.

There is no contradiction in Serge between the committed man of action and the poet. As a "professional revolutionary" (he would have preferred the more modest title of *militant*), his career united the roles of propagandist, organizer, journalist, agitator, theoretician, pamphleteer, translator, publicist, militiaman, manual worker, occasional secret agent, and political prisoner (for a total of more than ten years in five different countries!). His political commitments evolved from anarchism through syndicalism, Bolshevism, and Trotskyism to a kind of socialist humanism. Yet it is as a witness and ultimately as an artist that he will be remembered.

Born in 1890 in Brussels, Victor Kibalchich (Serge was a pseudonym) inherited the spiritual values of the Russian revolutionary emigration from his parents and carried them through both defeated and victorious movements: the Socialist Young Guards of Belgium (which he joined at the age of thirteen); the "tragic bandits" of 1911 French anarchism (out of solidarity with whom he was condemned to five years in the penitentiary); the insurrectionary Spanish syndicalists of 1917; the Bolsheviks (whom he joined soon after his arrival in Civil War Russia in 1919); the organizers of the early Comintern; the irreducible Left Oppositionists who maintained their anti-Stalinist commitment through deportation and beyond; the betrayed and defeated POUM of the Spanish revolution; and finally the independent socialists during the years of World War II and exile.

Unique survivor of what in one poem he calls this "Constellation of Dead Brothers," Serge was a committed, fraternal, lucid witness who lived to incarnate their often tragic experience in works rich in ideas and human values, of which his poetry is perhaps the most intimate and condensed expression.

And what poetry! Serge was a writer of universal culture, though entirely self-educated. Thoroughly conversant with both French and Russian poetry, he could recite effortlessly and endlessly from memory (a faculty that must have saved his sanity more than once in prison). In his own verse we find echoes of Baudelaire, Sully Prudhomme, Rimbaud, Mallarmé, Péguy, Verhaeren, Jéhan Rictus, and a musicality evocative of Apollinaire and especially of Verlaine. Serge's son, the painter Vlady, recalls him "singing" his poems. Receptive to every mode of poetic invention, he was on intimate terms with the Surrealists Breton and Péret (with whom he shared his final exile), and Octavio Paz reports that Serge was the first to reveal the work of Henri Michaux and Valéry Larbaud, then unknown in Mexico.

However, the richness of Serge's poetic vision goes beyond French letters. It embraces a larger world of history, geography, and class struggle refracted through the specifically Russian literary tradition of spirituality, philosophical depth, and social consciousness. A Russian spirit expressing himself in the purest French, Serge depicts himself (in the poem "Frontier") as a "torn man, a Eurasian." His writing fused two cultures with a mastery comparable only to that of a Conrad or a Nabokov.

Serge's association with the Russian poetry of his time was intimate. As early as 1909, we find him eking out a precarious living in Paris translating Russian novels and the poetry of Artzybashev, Balmont, and Merezhkovsky. In 1917, attempting to cross into Russia to join the revolutionaries, he struck up a friendship with Nikolai Stepanovich Gumilov, already a famous poet, who was on his way to join the Whites. "I am a traditionalist, monarchist, imperialist and pan-Slavist," declared Gumilov. "Mine is the true Russian nature, just as it was formed by Orthodox Christianity. You also have the true Russian nature, but at its opposite extreme, that of spontaneous anarchy, primitive violence, and unruly belief. I love all of Russia, even what I want to fight in it, even what you represent. . . . " In 1921 Serge was to struggle vainly trying to stop the Cheka from shooting this friend and adversary whose face and verses were to haunt him for years.

From the time of his arrival in revolutionary Russia during the terrible winter of 1918-1919, Serge was in contact with poets and writers, and his *Memoirs*, along with the articles on Soviet literary life he penned for the French magazine *Clarté*, provide fascinating portraits of poets like Alexander Blok, Andrei Biely, Sergei Yesenin, Osip Mandelstam, Boris Pasternak, and Vladimir Mayakovsky, as well as penetrating analysis and appreciation of their work.

Unlike Gumilov, who had openly conspired against the regime, the attitude toward the revolution of most of the outstanding poets of the pre-war generation was more conciliatory. Yet Serge's accounts of his relations with them are also tinged with anguish. The epic spirit of the revolution, he wrote in 1922,* had sparked new creative impulses among the poets, whether of Christian, symbolist, or futurist inspiration. Citing Biely's "Christ is Reborn" (which Serge first translated into French), Blok's mythic vision of a "Christ crowned with roses" who, "invisible and silent," walks in the snow storm before "The Twelve" Red Guards with their pointed caps and rifles, and Mayakovsky's grandiose "150,000,000," he concluded: "To understand these times, hearts and minds must rise to the level of epic. The fact is that there is a profound lyricism in the revolution, that it is a new faith, that it at every moment teaches the sacrifice of old, diminished, worn-out, obsolete values for new values . . . at times exalting the individual to an irresistible feeling of greatness. . . . " Serge own poems of the period ("City," 1920, and "Max," 1921) reflect this mood.

With increasing anguish, however, Serge witnessed the gradual extinction of the creative outpouring of this heroic period under the pressures of conformity, falseness, and corruption. "What can I do now in this life?" Biely asked him despondently one evening. "I cannot live outside this Russia of ours and I cannot breathe within it." We find something of the same sentiment in Serge's poem, "The Asphyxiated Man." While Serge had viewed the Red Terror during the Civil War as an unavoidable necessity (all the while protesting against its excesses, as we have seen in the case of Gumilov), he considered its perpetuation into the succeeding period of relative calm to be "an immense and demoralizing blunder."

By the mid-twenties, Serge found himself surrounded by suicides: first the Communist militants protesting the stifling of inner-Party debate and driven to despair by pervasive bureaucratization and corruption, then the poets: "The telephone rings: 'Come quickly, Yesenin has killed himself.' I run out in the snow. I enter his room in the Hotel International, and I can hardly recognize him; he no longer looks himself. . . . "

Serge remarked that "Yesenin had tried to be in tune with the times, and with our official literature." As Yesenin wrote, "I am a stranger in my own

---

*"*Les Ecrivains russes et la révolution*," *Clarté*, Vol. 1922, pp.387-390.

land. . . . " "My poems are no longer needed now, and I myself am out of place. . . . " "I am not a new man, I have one foot in the past, and yet I wish, I the stumbler, the cripple, to join the cohort of steel once more." Yesenin's last verses, written in his own blood, echo throughout this collection of Serge's: "There is nothing new about dying in this life/ But there is surely nothing new about living either."

Mayakovsky, who was soon to put a bullet through his own heart, had addressed a reproachful farewell to Yesenin. Serge depicts Mayakovsky's "athletic body straining with a sort of jeering violence, hammering out his farewell before audiences for whom [Yesenin's] death was turning into a symbol: " 'This planet's not well equipped for joy, Joy must be wrenched from future times!' "

In 1924, Serge had devoted a long article in *Clarté* to his appreciation of Mayakovsky's genius, tempered by reservations about Mayakovsky's futurism with its "hyperbole," "decadent iconoclasm," and "egocentrism" (criticisms which Mayakovsky disdainfully rejected during their only serious conversation). At the time of Mayakovsky's suicide in 1930 Serge wrote: "He wasted his best talents in a weary quest for God knows what ideological line, demanded of him by petty pedants who made a living out of it. Having become the most-requested rhymster of hack journalism, he allowed his personality to be sacrificed to this daily drudgery."

Serge saw "the gigantic scale of certain royalties" during the period of economic liberalism known as the NEP as a corrupting influence encouraging the worst kind of official literary conformity, which many writers, to their credit, did their best to resist. The advent of the Stalinist Terror spelled the doom of any real originality or independence. In "The Writer's Conscience,"* published shortly before his death in 1947, Serge evokes his recollection of a literary soiree at the home of Osip Mandelstam in 1932 during which the poet read out a recently completed nature poem and asked his friends if they thought it was "publishable." Mandelstam was trying to write "safe" poetry, but the voice of freedom within him was so strong that he couldn't censor it. For Serge, Mandelstam's "visions of Lake Erivan and the snows of Mount Ararat awakened, like a murmuring breeze, a call for freedom, a subversive praise of the imagination, an affirmation of ungovernable thought." We find these same images with the same resonance in Serge's poem, "Tiflis."

Within a few months, Serge was arrested and deported, shortly followed by Mandelstam, who apparently died in the camps. What enrages Serge in "The Writer's Conscience" is the "universal cowardice" of Western writers and intellectuals who remained silent throughout an entire decade during which

---

*Reprinted in David Craig, ed. *Marxists on Literature, An Anthology,* Penguin, 1975.

writers like Mandelstam, Pilniak, and Babel, personally known to them and translated into every language, were massacred. "No PEN Club, even those that held banquets for them, asked the least question about their fate." While acknowledging the courage of the poets of the anti-Nazi Resistance (Aragon and Eluard) and the Sartrian concept of "committed" literature, Serge (whose *Resistance* poems date from 1935) cannot hide his indignation: "The fact that this poetry is signed by poets who, in other circumstances, sang the praises of the executioners and the torturers, insulted the victims, spread lies on the graves of another Resistance motivated by the same goals — the defense of man against tyranny — leads us, by a terrible alchemy, to the negation of all the values they affirm."

We find this same indignation, controlled by a rigorous irony, in poems like "The Death of Panaït Istrati": "You lay upon your press clippings, like Job upon his ashes /quietly spitting the last bit of your lungs /in the faces of those copy-pissers,/ glorifiers of profitable massacres,/profiteers of disfigured revolutions . . . " and in the plight of "The Asphyxiated Man," a Civil War partisan dying neglected and abandoned, his courageous past exploited by " . . . good authors,/servile glory-hounds" making "memorable books and scenarios out of it."

The striking fact that emerges from this rapid survey of Serge's participation in the bright beginning, gradual corruption, and ultimate tragic massacre of the Soviet poetic movement is that Serge alone, by dint of his unbending opposition and his special status as a French-language writer, was able to continue writing and to write *freely.* He spoke the truth aloud and perpetuated the spiritual traditions of the Russian revolutionary intelligentsia at the very moment when the voices of his Russian colleagues were forced into silence. Thus his writings, and especially this collection of poems written in deportation on the Ural, represent a unique strand of continuity between a lost generation and what one hopes will be a new beginning, with "no blank pages," in Soviet literature.

Indeed, by a fitting irony that Serge, whose motto was "nothing is ever lost," would certainly have savored, the Soviets are publishing for the first time in Russian, Serge's epic novel of the Great Purges, *The Case of Comrade Tulayev,* in, of all places, the magazine, *URAL* (Vol. 1989, Jan.-Mar.)!

Serge wrote the bulk of the poems forming the present collection in semi-captivity on the Ural River, at Orenburg, to which he was deported in 1933 after 80 days of solitary confinement and interrogation at Moscow's notorious Lubianka prison. Orenburg, the once-prosperous provincial capital of the Kazakhs (or Kirghiz), a nomadic people of the Central Asian steppes, was in the throes of a hideous famine when Serge arrived there. Soon he was followed by his thirteen-year-old son, Vlady, and his wife, Liouba, who had been driven permanently insane by the Stalinist persecutions. Gainful employment was out of the question as long as Serge maintained his attitude of opposition, and the struggle for bread and firewood was a daily preoccupation. When the political police (GPU) cut off Serge's correspondence with France — the source of his royalties — they nearly starved. Serge was carried off to the hospital where he would have died had not a letter containing money been allowed through.

During this period GPU had gathered at Orenburg a number of deportees who belonged, like Serge, to the Left Opposition: Communists (all expelled from the Party, of course) who stood with Leon Trotsky for inner-party democracy and internationalism, in opposition to the Stalinist bureaucratic dictatorship with its narrow nationalism, forced collectivization of peasants, and insanely rapid forced industrialization. Some were old Bolsheviks who had fought in the revolutions of 1905 and 1917; others had joined the Party during the Civil War. All were distinguished by a courage and integrity that had brought them, by a tragic irony of history, from the summits of power which they had wrested from the hands of Czarist reaction as leaders of the revolutionary masses, back to the condition of persecuted, exiled, and imprisoned rebels under the new reaction that had taken power in Russian in the name of "Communism."

Serge immortalized them in a fictionalized form in his 1939 novel, *Midnight in the Century*, which is largely based on his Orenburg experience. All of them perished during the Stalinist blood purges, which began with the first Moscow Trial in the summer of 1936. Unlike the Communists who, out of fear, Party loyalty, or despair, reviled themselves and cooperated in the bloody farce of the show trials (see Serge's poem "Confessions"), they remained loyal to their principles even unto death. "I have described these men," wrote Serge, "because I am grateful to them for having existed, and because they incarnated an epoch." It is to them that *Resistance* is dedicated.

In the spring of 1936, thanks to the dogged protests of his comrades in France and the intervention of André Gide and Romain Rolland, Serge was liberated ("a miracle of solidarity," he called it) and allowed to return with his family to Europe. However, all his manuscripts (including two completed novels) were illegally confiscated on the Polish border by the political police and never returned.* Serge was able to reconstruct his poems from memory, and they were published in Paris in 1938. They bear the mark of the time and place of their composition:

---

*Serge had obtained for his writings an exit permit from the official censor, *GLAVLIT*, and deposited no fewer than seven painstakingly-typed copies with institutions and friends. Today, under glasnost, the official Foundation for Soviet Culture has agreed to search for them. Might Serge's tenacity and long-term historical optimism see another "miracle?"

"I was finishing my books in a state of uncertainty," wrote Serge. "What would their destiny be, and mine? ... By one of those strokes of irony that are so frequent in Russia, the Soviet Press was, quite appropriately, commemorating an anniversary of the Ukranian national poet Taras Shevchenko, who in 1847 had been exiled for ten years to the steppes of Orenburg, 'forbidden to draw or to write.' He did, all the same, write some clandestine poetry which he concealed in his boots. In this report I had an overwhelming insight into the persistence in our Russian land, after a century of reform, progress, and revolution, of the same willful determination to wipe out the rebellious intelligence without mercy. Never mind, I told myself, I must hold on: hold on and work on, even under this slab of lead."

Serge's determination is evident in poems like "Be Hard," "Trust," and "Stenka Razin." But the overwhelming feeling in the Orenburg poems is one of fraternity — of identity and communion with the land, with its people, and ultimately with the universe itself. For Serge, "he who speaks, he who writes is above all one who speaks on behalf of all those who have no voice" — the people "On the Ural River," "Old Woman," "The Asphyxiated Man," and the whole "Constellation of Dead Brothers," which includes the companions-in-exile to whom *Resistance* is dedicated. On another level, writing for Serge is at once defiance and acceptance of death: "first of all, a need to capture, to fix, to understand, to interpret, to recreate life" and then "a quest for poly-personality, a means of living several destinies, of penetrating other people and communicating with them."

Although this definition of writing is common to Balzac and other creators, in Serge's conception there is a generosity, a peculiar tenderness, as in the poem "Cassiopeia" where he calls on his lover, the young nurse Tatiana, to give herself to an anonymous dead man with whose spirit he has merged: "he no longer has anything but our warmth, he has only my arms to embrace you." As the poem ends, Serge invokes the cosmos itself which "unites" him eternally to the unknown dead man through "the risen stars and this sign between us: the high glittering triangles of Cassiopeia."

Indeed, there is a pervasive sense of communion and an attitude of prayer in the poetry of this doctrinaire Marxist whose basic attitude of solidarity with humanity and the universe expands into what might be termed a "materialist spirituality." It begins with the simple act of witness, of recording and sharing the lives and sufferings of his comrades, the defiant and doomed revolutionaries, or of a dying man, an old woman grinding chalk, a poor fisherman, or four young women fording the Ural. The unromantic but deeply felt reality of these portraits of men and women seized in the nexus of history, geography, and economics lends them a nobility which is their beauty.

But for Serge, who is unashamed to refer to himself as "the Son of man" in one of his poems, the act of witness takes on an almost Christian sense of voluntarily shared suffering, of acceptance and refusal of inevitable evil. If for Serge the Marxist, human consciousness is the "soul" of the material universe, then for Serge the poet, writing is the expression of that soul. The starting point of the poem is always a concrete evocation of individuals rooted in the often harsh realities of their historical situation, yet Serge's universalist perspective explodes the work outward into time and space. Thus "Tiflis," a poem rich in local color, leaps from the bazaars and mosques of an Oriental city to the vision of the "glaciers of Elbrus and Kazbek" and from there to that of "the nameless mountains of the only necessary continents — O absolute deserts, O fertile continents of consent and refusal!"

The Sergian sense of human striving, suffering, and solitude somehow "rescued " through solidarity and consciousness in the cosmos is nowhere better expressed than in his final poem, "Hands," which is among other things a meditation on his own death. Beginning with the "astonishing contact" between the veins of his own hands and those of an old man in a 16th-century terra-cotta, Serge arrives at a vision of unity transcending time, space, and ultimately death, "A drop of blood — a single ray of light falls from one hand to the other, dazzling."

Serge's son and companion-in-exile, the artist Vlady, to whom we owe thanks for the magnificent drawings that illustrate this volume and for his invaluable help in interpreting his father's poems, relates the final irony of Serge's life as follows:

"One day in November of 1947 my father brought a poem to my house in Mexico City. Not finding me at home, he left to take a walk downtown. From the Central Post Office, he mailed me the poem. A short while later, he died in a taxi. That night a friend came to bring me the news. I found him on an operating table in the police station. A yellowish lamp illuminated the sinister room. The first thing I noticed were his shoes: they had holes in them. This shocked me, for he was careful about his dress, although his clothes were always of the cheapest. The following day, I was unable to draw his face, for they had put a plaster death-mask over it. I limited myself to drawing his hands, which were beautiful. A few days later I received his poem: 'Hands.' "

Mexico, February 1989

viii

FRONTIER

On the banks of the Ural River
the woods are beginning to turn silver, the river is dozing on the
    sand,
the kite is soaring—
yet not as high as the pursuit plane
that heedlessly loops the loop of death on the golden fringes of a
    white cloud,
or briskly skirts
a terrestial abyss deeper than the stellar abyss.

Here is where Europe ends, the frontier of a world
for which the Atlantic is only an inland sea
and Atlantis a memory.
Seven a.m.: it's eight p.m. at the other end of Greater Europe,
in Frisco, San Francisco, on the Pacific, on the frontier of the next,
    greater war,
Frisco where the IWWs live.
Whose eyes turned toward Asia stare at the ocean over there,
sad as my eyes from sounding this tangible nothingness of the
    beginning and end of continents
through the silence of the other human face?

The steppe begins with innocent plains,
with the purity of plains, the fertility, the immensity of plains
and the touch of naked earth offered to the skies.
Free attraction of spheres, space,
gallop of red ponies toward the source of every spring.

The vanquished wheat comes to an end, the sand dunes rise,
a scarlet sun atrociously consumes them,
O thirst, eternity, conflagration, bones,
vanity of vanities!

The Kirgiz camel driver has stopped singing—
immobile, blazing madness of sand,
mirages—when will the stars come out,
and do they exist?
Will there ever again be a single evening's mildness,
a night's coolness,
the unbelievable delight of a stagnant pond for a camel driver's
    throat,
a dog's rough tongue,
a camel's tortured mouth?

Silence absorbs the reach.

The primordial clay is coral red,
the sun hammers in dreadful red nails,
and that's where people saw a strange crimson beast running,
goaded by all the suffering on earth.
Its immeasurable flanks blocked out the whole horizon.

(And you know, the earth suffers more than hell—
hell was never more than a delirious mirage
of the children of the earth.)

When the Uzbek hunter, the sheep's avenger,
captures a wolf alive, he ties it up and, singing to himself,
lightly flays it, being very careful
to spare the arteries;
he flays it and then throws it out onto the steppe.

People claim
that a well-flayed wolf can run quite some time,
bleeding in the desert,
run and run toward a prodigious stream of the Kara Kumy,
the Milky Way,
to quench its unimaginable thirst.

The mirage magnifies its image erected
flickering

above the still-smoking lava of chaos.
A shepherd's eyes enclose this image in legend forever,
this legend I am presenting on the frontier of Asia,
on the frontier of Europe,
I who feel like a man torn apart, a Eurasian.

ON THE URAL RIVER

In winter the people of this land keep warm by burning the kiziak
they make out of cow dung gathered on the steppe and dried in the
    sun,
it's an ancient task for woman and beast.
Elsewhere, beautiful laughing women stomp ripe grapes and the
    fumes make them a little drunk, but they don't know they have
    sisters here.
Vast, vast horizons, pure, distant, and light,
soft grass under the hot, shimmering air,
vast, vast sky, forgotten, blinding sky impossible to look at,
a slender, bare-legged Tatiana stands up straight, turning slowly in
    warm manure,
and the cow turns round too at the end of its tether, woman and
    beast together, sweating,
strangers on the horizon.
Blue-black flies buzz around them in the stench,
the breathing of the beast is weary like a lament.
The young woman stops now and then and sings to herself in an
    undertone from the depths of her misery
about the man who came back from a distant prison
and found the woman he loved in bed with another man and killed
    them both with one blow of his ax—
now her voice turns softly heartrending:
"Othello!"
and it's just the lament of Bogdan the Convict,
last spring the story took place in a neighboring village,
and the spring before that in another,
this is a story for all time
"for in this world all men kill the thing they love . . ."
Dust, dust on Desdemona,
but a naked breast puts flowers on life . . .

Then there's the fisherman in the pond,
poorer than the poor man in Puvis' gray landscape,

this bony old man in the sparkling water.
He went in naked except for his short jacket and felt shepherd's hat
and hauled on the net—"Hey! hey! Kolka, pull harder, in God's
    name!"
The thin, naked child struggled on the opposite shore.
Living silver commas suddenly darted about their legs in the mud.
"Catch them, catch them, boy!"
Lord, there's nothing miraculous about this fishing; Lord, it's a
    miracle that anyone can live on it!

Red granite outcrops through the red clay,
the world's first days show in the pain of living,
the street wanders off, huddled under its tottering, tumble-down
    houses like old women squatting in the sun,
it takes up scant room between the sky and the endless steppe,
a ragged Kirgiz walks alone, mournfully pursued by the dogs'
    barking,
nothing to steal, nothing to eat, lousy beggar! and even the dogs
    know you're hungry . . .
I met his black look from the depths of time,
he's gone past, it's the past.

Here I am at my table where some pages are begun, tense
pages that wanted to live and already feel lost, alone before these
stifled pages
with this ton of lead on the back of my neck and worry.
What is happening in Asturias?
Let's get to work. The naked fisherman dragging his net in the
    pond did not see those traces of sky that I saw.
Let's get to work so that one day, perhaps, a passerby might see
in the lines ripening at this moment, as I too haul in my net in the
    pond of useless days,
some traces of a reassuring sky that I cannot see there.

Orenburg, summer 1935

OLD WOMAN

This old woman walking under her yoke
laden with unnamable things
casts a shadow like a caricature of a horse,
a poor nag
whose head hangs by a thread.

The ancients denied that such a being had a soul,
immortal or not.
Hardly equipped with one themselves, scholars
gravely pondered the question.

Today, plaster saints and others in lyrical terms
would call you sister.
Old woman,
you don't even suspect their comfortable lie,
it's a thousand million leagues away
from your heavy, numb steps sunk in the black earth.

The truth squishes out beneath your steps
in your wet shadow
that smells of manure.

You can no longer be saved.
Just think! Seventy years old,
and it's too late.
And maybe six hundred and seventy years of servitude,
or more.
It's too early.

SOMEWHERE ELSE

Midnight, and I'm smoking in the shed with the snow-corroded
    roof.
The Milky Way shines through the cracks.
Around this squatting old woman move the giant shadows of old
    servants,
serfs that were beaten and sold . . .
She has powerful, tenacious hands that in the darkness work over
    the desolate whiteness,
severely, obstinately,
since the beginning of time,
crushing with light taps the chalk she'll mold near dawn.
The granite vibrates slightly under the mute pounding,
isn't this the beating of the old exhausted heart of this land?

I speak out loud, between long stretches of silence, words almost
    devoid of sense,
in order to fill the void between us, old woman,
the void of appearances,
for under my breath I tell you things that astonish me but that you
    couldn't understand.
If Orion's Belt suddenly fell to earth in a rain of burning stars,
wouldn't you think that the end of the world had come?
"Lord, have mercy on our fields!
All these fallen stars will only bring people worse luck!"

Somewhere else, grandmother, there are attractive women who are
gracious, perfumed, pampered, loved, and loving;
they will never know anything about your pain, about your hunger,
about these shadows where you toil—
there are elegant men speaking to them with intelligent gestures
about the Oedipus complex, about the aesthetic sense, about
    consciousness, and even about the proletariat;
somewhere tonight there is a happy Angelita—
"*Querida Angelita, amiga mía, tanto querida!*"

Somewhere else there are . . .
This grandmother answers me in her harsh voice, worn out by
    swamp fevers,
that you can't get the good crumbly chalk you used to,
that the Sakmara is going to overflow and the fields will be flooded,
and that life is hard, always hard—"And you have no idea how long
    it lasts."
And her hands
work, work, work
in eternity.

FOUR GIRLS

Four happy girls enter the water to ford the Ural River,
the spangled, sparkling, and welcoming water.
The water grasps the hard calves of these hikers from the edge of
     the steppes,
an invisible, soberly caressing hand
takes their knees, then the water's brisk coolness
weds their legs to rise and brush their secret flesh,
making a short shrill laugh tremble on their lips,
a laugh
that tastes like bitter fruit
in the mouth of a thirsty man.
Under her little red chintz dress the first one stretches a young body
that evokes an Athenian Victory with her slightly pointed breasts.
She has hair cut short on the nape, a high forehead, an arm
     outstretched,
the hand horizontal, and that already strong hand of a hardworking
     virgin
seems to point toward a summit,
an island,
a city
on the other side of the world where there is only *ordre,*
beauté,
luxe, calme et volupté
—but she's only showing the way to a linden rustling with nests
on the other shore.
Will she, a serf scarcely freed, poorly freed, ever know
how to name beauty,
she who sees so clearly the tranquil landscape of which she is
at this moment
the youthful living heart?

Another girl, with a stocky figure, has the shoulders of a sixteen-
     year-old
that recall the graceful awkwardness of animals,

colorful shawls, and furs under the tent made of hides.
She must have little black eyes, without lashes and almost without
    brows,
the close, white teeth of carnivores,
her flat face seems firm and hard, with round cheekbones—
in the thirteenth century Khulagu Khan's archers had the same
    cheekbones,
teeth, dark eyes, and tight smile as this child
when they crossed the river coming the other way,
in triumph.

The last two girls laugh as they stumble against each other,
sisters, friends, pals—I can't see their faces;
their backs arch against the green reflections of the foliage.
What party, what love, what desire, what pleasure are they talking
    about to have that tinkling, bell-like laughter?
Probably none; they're laughing just
because it's a nice day.
I won't see them again except in other girls, I won't recognize them
if I see them dancing one evening to the sounds of a brass band.
They are certainly not beautiful and have no special charm,
no more genius than a blossoming flower,
no more pride,
no more kindness
(but is any more needed?).
They are four girls among many, like all others, four human
    figurines
molded by the moment,
released from the common fate, returned to it
as to a lover.

I know that they will not have their promised joy,
happiness is not on the other side of the river,
the other face of the world will stay closed to them,
their future has the monotonous color of the plains.

Far away now, almost gone, where are they,
the four laughing girls of a moment ago?

They are on the other shore, four real girls
from my village of exile
and their image has not faded in me.

THE ASPHYXIATED MAN

Green bushes are bursting with giant flowers,
on the doorstep of the small hospital made of gray boards
there are these sleeping flowers
that smell of chloroform.

A nurse dressed in white is seated on the steps,
she's a brunette with the wide eyes of the plains,
she cracks sunflower seeds between her teeth.

The patient, squatting on the ground in an oversize shirt, where his
      uncelebrated martyr's body totters,
stretches his bony neck; his face has a strange gray color,
he looks like a drowned man badly drowned, badly fished out, and
      sent on his way,
it is the face of asphyxiation, of the terror
of the last days,
pierced by eyes anterior to any possible resurrection.
His hoarse breathing shoos the buzzing flies,
I see the veins throb in his neck.
His other-worldly eyes cry out to me that there is no more air:
"Citizen! What have they done with all the air?"

Two high-breasted girls stop in front of this asphyxiated man.
The one in a sailor's jacket and with an anchor and a lover's name
      tattooed on her bare arm
and who has her hair cut short and sensual pink nostrils
says to her friend:
"He's done for, dear. Oh my, what an ugly death's head!"
She puts her arm around her friend's frail shoulders.
"Let's go, Charlotte!" she says.

The flier who fell at dawn from seventh heaven, in a parachute,

and who knows that there's air to drown in, to break up in, air, air to
    fall in,
kilometers of air and fear to cross without flinching
to die or to obtain the certificate, first-class rations, and that
    knowledge of the sky that is no more than a new ignorance of
    the heavens—
the flier's eyes follow the young women.
"There's nothing anyone can do for the poor old guy now. There's
    no point in even looking at him. Let's go, girls."

He would like to dance tonight in Linden Gardens with the
    tattooed girl of the sensual pink nostrils,
he would suddenly take her breasts in his hands—
"You're a great kid and I could buy you some silk stockings, y'know,
we're the happy youth of the birth of socialism."

Believers say that Christ died on the cross for you,
it hardly shows.
The Savior botched your salvation.

The lecturers at the Atheists Club say that revolutions are made to
    save you and people like you.
You'd hardly know that, either,
and yet all those important people are very positive,
all those healthy people.

Your papers prove that you fought to save yourself
with Chapaev, with Furmanov, with my friend Mitia, the deported
    wino,
down the Ural River stripped by dawns—
but even that didn't do you any good.

And your blood burning from the civil wars, your partisan's
    seething rage,
all that would be lost, poor folk, if there weren't good authors,
servile glory hounds, good money makers
to get memorable books and scenarios out of it.

The nurse has finished munching her seeds, she has gone away.
The asphyxiated man remains alone among the green bushes
in the dazzling light, colors, and pain,
alone in the universe,
alone in the pure, inaccessible, unbreathable azure,
where his black mouth vainly begs for air.

Luminous disks descend, ascend, explode there
and I am here, dressed in white, eye sockets framed in gold, useless,
I, the only person conscious of his suffering and death,
I, the last, impotent human face he'll ever see,
I who have nothing for him but this absurd remorse.

Orenburg, summer 1935

TIFLIS

Kurdish women in red dresses, the donkey ambling down a narrow
    street in Maydan,
chance colors, their strange dozes, their rousings among the shifting
    arabesques of the bazaar,
leather collars around the necks of little barbarian girls, Tartar
    women
who sell ripe grapes and hot peppers,
steam from boiling water spouting from subterranean lava
for the Orbeliani Baths, pay three rubles and be pure.

Two short-legged oxen, stocky and stubborn, split the crowd, their
    gray horns thrust forward,
they patiently haul the old two-wheeled cart that dates from the
    time of Tamerlane.
A man dressed in homespun drives them; he's just as stocky, just as
    stubborn as they, a Mingreli man,
the only difference is he can sing the poems of Rustaveli.

In the blue mosque of Shah Abbas, covered with brilliant faience,
an unknown captive walked with a light step between unsheathed
    sabers,
preceded by an invisible hope.
His sandals trod the dust, as they might have trod the foamy crests
    of the sea.
From the square windows of Metekh Prison, faces of the earth,
those nearest heaven
it would seem,
could see him go out,
go out and return.

The Georgian tombs of the Monastery of St. David lie on the border
    between presence and the void,
the flesh-colored alabaster stones endlessly reveal
so much carnal freshness that they truly testify to eternal life

15

where a person's name, face, pain, and even memory fade.

From the heights of Mt. David I saw the glaciers of Elbrus, Kazbek,
and more distant, icier, clearer,
Ararat, Pamir, Everest, the Andes,
and more distant, icier, clearer,
above the gently oscillating green fields the dazzling summits of the
    realest mountains:
these are the nameless mountains of the only necessary
    continents—
O absolute deserts, O fertile continents of consent and refusal!

Orenburg, 1935

A CRIME IN TIFLIS

Why was he drinking Imeretia wine,
the man with a moneybag who came from Kutais
with his old heart worn down like a Kurdistan carpet
on which people had traded, suffered, danced,
trampled on promises and stabbed someone,
so poorly loved, so sound asleep?

Why did he like the girl whose heart-rending song
deceived him like life
and tempted him like the night?

He would have wanted to fall into the rivers of stars,
O cool Milky Way, Andromeda, Pleiades, Cassiopeia!
fall toward you, be no more than falling, explosion, flowing, calm,
but he fell with the weight of flesh, pain, and the tomb,
through the narrow window, just thirty meters, with his aorta
lightly pierced.

The phosphorescent waters foamed in the depths of the drowned
    firmament,
washed his wounds, swept away his body, so cruelly crushed.
But in the morning,
Tamaras were rinsing out their laundry on the banks of the Kura;
these lovers with childlike glances had supple arms that the water
    caressed
better than love ever did;
the murdered man dropped into the depths of their eyes,
for they thought they recognized him without knowing him,
they mourned him without loving him, laid him in the ground,
and then smiled at the living and soon forgot him.

Orenburg, 1935

HISTORY OF RUSSIA

I

The very quiet,
the very gentle,
the very pious Czar Alexis Mikhailovitch,
would wash his hand after a foreigner kissed it.

The chronicle reports that like a good Christian he fasted
three days out of seven.
Which didn't prevent his dying obese after having ordered,
like a gentle czar,
a great deal of torture.

He's depicted with a tawny beard, fresh complexion, smooth brow,
deep in his cunning eyes a fleeting reddish glint,
under the pointed hat edged with white fur.
He loved pearls, brocade, Isfahan silks,
gold, silver, precious stones;
once a year he held a celebration for the poor.
Good paupers, may your wounds redeem his sins
of evil thoughts, lust, greed,
and a few superfluous massacres.
God knows that most of them are justified and that I am a merciful
    czar.
Poor people, even if you know that he's lying,
eat and drink your fill, if your wounds did not redeem the powerful,
what would they be good for?

He chose his wife from the loveliest girls in the land.
Intrigue dumped before this redoubtable fiancé a pale Ophelia,
half-strangled by her braids.

They deported her father, on account of the hope, fear, and mortal
    anguish the virgin had suffered.
Intrigue brought pure-hearted Natalia to him

and she was destined to carry in her belly Peter of the hard heart—
    born of an unknown father.
He was a better husband and father than Czar Ivan Vassilievitch the
    Terrible
and his own nominal son Peter Alexeievitch the Great
because he didn't kill with his own hand any of his own children
and had none of his wives tortured to death.

If he exiled his favorites, wasn't that the usual thing?
If he exiled the incorruptible patriarch and the unshakable
    heresiarch,
was it without love?
If he had the heretics burned in the northern forests,
wasn't it out of love?

Let's respect him as the wise politician
educated by riot,
the perspicacious monarch who, in his secret tête-à-tête with fright,
discovered the surest resources of power:
fear, denunciation, betrayal, espionage,
the moderate torture of strappado,
exile and deportation
to the polar regions, at the ends of the earth,
and he knew how to build on the dark mire of the human heart
his Chancellery of Secret Affairs,
an exemplary institution, all in all, O Holy Office!

No doubt his financial deals,
adroitly clinched with hangings,
were unfortunate
and smacked of counterfeiting,
inflation, bankruptcy, etc.,
—but weren't all the great kings, anointed by the Lord,
great counterfeiters?

In short, all he lacked to keep the reputation of a great monarch
was to be a little more intelligent,
a little better served,

a little more wicked,
and to have a little less need of cash.

II

Stenka Razin

In those days there lived—mighty through fire, blood, and the
    sword—
Another czar, known as the outlaw czar.
All along the Volga, our mother, he lit
The signal fires of a wild deliverance, bristling with scythes,
Gallows, and chopped-off heads.

Liberté, égalité, fraternité,
Name the fruits of the bitterest hope,
Avenge, avenge the blood spilled
On knives, on swords since time began.
Stenka the Just knew how to treat the masters
As the masters treat the slaves
And did not imagine that a better man could be born.
In the evenings the cossack girls in this village still sing
To the accompaniment of a guitar
The Lament of Stenka Razin; but what their fathers
And their uncles did, right here,
Just sixteen years ago
They've forgotten, let's forget it, guitar
Sing for their hearts,
Enchant oblivion, make the choirs
Tuned by oblivion sing.

A silver sickle rises in the July sky
Above the little red minaret of Orenpossad.
I listen to these shrill voices and the guitar
And the toads croaking in the pond.
I vaguely think, alone before the steppe,

Of all those the world over from whom I am not separated—
Of the unemployed in Amsterdam, of Tom Mooney in his
California prison
For fifteen or eighteen years, what do we know about it?
And who could tell the toll of such years?
Of the astonishing victory of the Saragossa general strike yesterday,
In June 1934,
Of the next Congress of the United Federation of Teachers,
Of the fresh grave—but are there flowers on it?—
Of the fresh grave of Koloman Wallisch,
Of the barred window—but are there flowers on it?—
Of his wife Paula in an Austrian prison.

The young voices rise knowing neither what they are singing about
Nor the living and the dead for whom they sing,
United, united through time, chains, space.
And when they announce the landing on distant riverbanks of
The shining boats of Stepan the Brigand,
The liberator,
The hero, the executioner of executioners,
The herald,
I see growing on the ripples of the water
The revivifying specter
Of a barbarous freedom drunk on its tears.

Stenka was broken alive on the wheel the sixth of June sixteen
        hundred and seventy,
In front of the Kremlin,
Before the Church of St. Basil the Blessed
And the Tower of the Savior.

While they are breaking his bones, Stenka yells at his cowardly,
        moaning brother,
"Shut up, dog!"
These are his last, proud words, his only words under the ax.
They cut through the bright pain of his hacked-off limbs,
The right arm, the left leg,
They flow from his lips, mixed with bloody saliva,

21

A crowd gathers them
in the disgusting stench
That stagnates under the scaffold.
History will preserve them like the words of Christ.

But dogs are not cowardly beasts.
Dogs maintain their canine dignity very well
In this bitch of a life.
And yet for centuries we have raised them in our image.

Cowardly brother, shut up!
Before the suffering of one stronger than you,
better than you, who,
Dying for you, dies more than you.

Orenburg, July 1934

III

Confessions

We have never been what we are,
the faces of our lives are not our own,
the voices that you hear, the voices that have spoken so loudly above
      the storm
are not our own,
nothing you have seen is true,
nothing we have done is true,
we are entirely different.

We have never thought our thoughts,
believed our faith,
willed our will,
today our only truth is despair,
this confession of a mad degeneration,

22

this fall into blackness
where faith is renounced and recovered one last time.

We have neither faces nor names, neither strength nor past
—for everything is over and done with
We should never have existed
—for everything is devastated
And it is we who are the guilty, we the unforgivable,
we the most miserable, we the most ruined,
it is we . . . know that
—and be saved!

Believe our confessions, join in our vow
of complete obedience; scorn our disavowals.
Once put down, the old revolt is nothing but obedience.

May those who are less devoted be proud,
may those who have forgiven themselves be proud,
may those who are more devoted be proud,
may those who have not given up be proud.

If we roused the peoples and made the continents quake,
shot the powerful, destroyed the old armies, the old cities, the old
    ideas,
began to make everything anew with these dirty old stones,
these tired hands, and the meager souls that were left us,
it was not in order to haggle with you now,
sad revolution, our mother, our child, our flesh,
our decapitated dawn, our night with its stars askew,
with its inexplicable Milky Way torn to pieces.

If you betray yourself, what can we do but betray ourselves with
    you?
After lives such as these, what possible death could there be, if not,
    in this betrayal, to die for you?

What more could we have done than kneel before you
in this shame and agony,

if in serving you we have called down upon you such darkness?

If others find in your heart stabbed a thousand times
the means to live on and to resist you in order to save you in twenty
    years,
a hundred years,
blessed are they by we who have never believed in benedictions,
blessed are they in our secret hearts
by we who can do nothing more.

We no longer belong to the future, we belong entirely to this age:
it is bloody and vile in its love for mankind,
we are bloody and vile like the men of this time.

Trample on us, insult us, spit on us,
vomit us,
massacre us,
our love is greater than this humiliation,
this suffering,
this massacre,
your iniquitous mouths are just, your mouths are our mouths,
we are in you,
your bullets are ours, and our mortal agony, our death, our infamy
    are yours,
and your vast life on these fields worked for centuries is forever
    ours!

Paris, October 12, 1938

BOAT ON THE URAL RIVER

Five men and one woman—
six in a boat.
Guess which is the deaf one, the blind,
the lost, the distraught,
the madman of silence
and the one whose soul dances
more lightly than his suffering,
presences and absences,
smiles in the depths of the water,
bars on the pale sky . . .

Men sing to cheat their night
when they are drunk.
We are steadfastly men
and more lucid than the drunkest.
We'll sing too: *Volga, Volga,*
here come Stenka's tall, bright boats . . .

The river slowly undulates
—red rocks, steppe, woods—
what is weeping in our voices,
what is groaning,
what is singing in our hearts?

Arise, workers of the world!
hey! hey!
the haulers pull on the rope,
the rope around the neck.

Sing, Alexis, your number's up
old insurgent
with a coolie's mug,
life is heavy.

Row, Vassili, row. Let's pull together
we are brothers
in defeat and hard times—
our defeat is prouder and greater
than their lying victory . . .
It's good to go up the rivers
as long as your back's not broken . . .
We'll hold on as long as we can.

Kiss the girl you fancy . . .

Jacques lightly purses his thin lips
like a wise Jew who will live to grow old.
Boris with the profile of a hungry wolf
drinks in the sadness of a night without drink.
No one doubts you, my friend,
if you're lost, what can anyone do?

Our days are short,
fill my glass . . .

The Gypsy girl or the Egyptian
grasps at a fleeting pleasure
(where are the thesis, the antithesis,
where is love, the divine synthesis?)
and dips her hands in the water
—against the current.

Twenty-six and eleven fell from the sky yesterday
blazing right into death.
Death of others, how light you are!
Happiness of others, how bitter you are!
Where are the troubled waters,
troubled like you?

Softly the chorus begins again—
no! sings out in this empty evening,

this evening without struggle or hope,
sings out one last time:

If the wind raises barricades,
if the paving stones shine like lightning,
before the people, comrades . . .

Night falls, the boat puts in,
stop singing.
Exile relights its captive lanterns
on the shore of time.
O solitudes, here we are
standing and free and willing,
faithful to what men are making
of these times.

Orenburg, May 20, 1935

(About a boat ride that we took, six deported communists.)

27

TETE-A-TETE

I am sane, but there are times when I feel I've gone mad,
my psychiatry text has nothing to say about that,
the specialists would say: "It's funny, but you seem normal,
those are just ideas,
get some rest, friend,
and before you go to sleep at night, whisper
everything is okay, everything is okay, thirty-six times"—
and as the specialists were amiably talking to me,
pity would rise in me like a tide,
because I know they are mad.

As sane as I am, only the nut-cases would welcome me like a
          brother
with their definitive laughter
roared at the beginning of the world.

You whom they've welcomed, a ghost of yourself,
I see your face change, as if at the memory of a crime,
lighted from below by an inexpiable glow,
my woman friend, my enemy, enemy of yourself,
but you're the victim and your hate is your sentence.

My eyes are stone in flesh sockets,
and these stones hurt you,
these stones wound you,
because you think my eyes strip you and judge you,
but it's you who judge me, my poor ruthless woman,
and I the one stripped.

I feel the storm and rage born within you, no one can say
from where it comes, how it erupts, exceeding human boundaries,
inhuman
is this demented tempest where you're only a burning shadow,
where I am only a mask—a mask on a tomb.

The time is not as heavy as a ravaged mask.

And when your features calm down and brighten—O still living
    woman!—you say: "Oh, I would like a little peace . . ." and in
    that great word
peace there are already
gentle waves at dawn beneath nascent, innocent foliage,
a welcome, a presence, a fulfillment,
there is what is not, what will *never* be.
(We know it so well, you and I, everything is there:
my strength forever strained to the point of death,
your defeat forever feeding on itself.)

They are quite wrong to say the ideas of mad people are not
    rational,
because they go beyond our commonplace reasons for doing absurd
    things,
our petty reasons for blindness, dullness, satisfaction,
our unreasonable reasons for escaping from real anguish.

Old Sigmund Freud explains it in his delirium:
the Oedipus complex has a Gorgon's head.
Old Scardanelli answers old Sigmund:
Such is man and such is the splendor of life.

Orenburg, 1935

Author's note: Near the end of his life, Hölderlin, then a schizophrenic,
signed the name "Scardanelli" to poems dated a century before.

DIALECTIC

I

We were born
in the time of the first perfected machine guns;
They were waiting for us, these excellent perforators
of armor plate and brains haunted by spirituality . . .

Have no doubt, ever since we began to ply the trade of most
    unwilling victim
—almost since time began—
we've known how to quaff every bitter drink,
gall, hemlock (now out of fashion), the little glass of rum
before the guillotine . . .

Jamaica rum, tropical sap,
be gentle on the palate of the deathly pale guy
who's paying for the crime of others
and for ours,
and place in our mouths a little of the bitterness
that his mouth distills for the peace of the best men.

We know how to carry all the crosses, wooden crosses,
swastikas,
climbing a little calvary really isn't anything
for the thieves and christs that we all are.
We have courage.
Ecce homo proletarians
and intellectuals "of all trades."

And if it's necessary once more to go up against the wall
of the desperate Communards,
we'll be there!

No doubt somewhat despite ourselves, once the wine is poured,
    we'll

drink it.
Long live the Commune, here's to everybody, long live man!
Cream of the assassins, brass hats, Versaillais!
Watch out, Signor Capitan, on the last step
of the last cellar:
my check is cashed at the Cheka.

II

These are leaders of armies, big capitalists, great executioners?
Heroes of the battles of Polesye, Voluyy, and the Carpathians?
These are generals, these trembling old men on all fours, crying,
      with moist eyes
and clouded hearts?
These are Knights of St. George and St. Andrew?
Go ahead, then, St. Capitalist the Assassinated,
it's now your turn.
As for me, I couldn't care less if you don't know what the Marquis
      de Gallifet did.
I don't know anything, either; me, I'm just a foreman from
      Gorlovka
and I haven't read books.
But there is someone greater than us who's forgotten nothing.

III

By order of the Rev. Comm.
they perish in a ditch in Chernavka
under the sabres of metal-workers from Taganka,
miners from Kashtanka,
and an anarchist bleeding from the death of his dream.
They perish exactly like—on September 2, 1792,
at the Abbaye Prison—Messieurs Montmorin,
Sombreuil, and Rulhière, gentlemen of the king's chamber.
Throat-slitting makes a muffled sound, a mad, disgusting sound,
crowd noise, delirious and sinister sound of waves.
Bailiff Maillart consulted a big register.

"To the La Force Prison!" He wiped his face with the back of his
     gray hand,
oh, a firm hand is needed to serve the first republic!
At dusk Citizen Billaud came to harangue the killers:
"*Sans culottes!* Brutus, Cinna, the glory of Rome,
the revolution will live in centuries of centuries to come,
the Commune sends you a barrel of good wine."

IV

"See," said the young, freckle-faced propagandist,
"see how materialist history repeats itself."

V

You've taught us so well the dirty trade practiced by the strongest
that in the end we will become masters at it.
We will have pounding hearts, pulsing brows,
eyes full of horrible images like remorse . . .
And then let them bury us and forget us
let nothing begin again and let the earth flourish . . .

Let's go, let's go, let's go!

Orenburg, 1935

BE HARD *(fragment)*

Not one new word germinates for you, comrade,
your problem has no solution,
your problem is made of reinforced concrete, with a steel armature,
and we are inside.

Let's be hard, as hard as chains, in time flesh will wear out chains,
in time the mind will make chains snap,
in time and with Bickford fuses, of course, and the precision
    clockwork
of machines that are mistakenly called infernal—for the
others are more infernal—
we will need time, flesh, intelligence, techniques, we will certainly
    need them:

let's be hard for a long time.

(And you! Be hard after we're gone! And pass on the word till the
    end of time!)

CONSTELLATION OF DEAD BROTHERS

André who was killed in Riga,
Dario who was killed in Spain,
Boris whose wounds I dressed,
Boris whose eyes I closed.

David, my bunk mate,
dead without knowing why
in a quiet orchard in France—
David, your astonished suffering
—six bullets for a 20-year-old heart . . .

Karl, whose nails I recognized
when you had already turned to earth,
you, with your high brow and lofty thoughts,
what was death doing with you!
Dark, tough human vine.

The North, the waves, the ocean
capsize the boat, the Four, now pallid,
drink deeply of anguish,
farewell to Paris, farewell to you all,
farewell to life, God damn it!

Vassili, throughout our sleepless midnights
you had the soul of a combatant
from Shanghai,
and the wind effaces your tomb
in the cornfields of Armavir.

Hong Kong lights up, hour of tall buildings,
the palm resembles the scimitar,
the square resembles the cemetery,
the evening is sweltering and you are dying,
Nguyên, in your prison bed.

And you, my decapitated brothers,
the lost ones, the unforgiven,
the massacred, René, Raymond,
guilty but not denied.

O rain of stars in the darkness,
constellation of dead brothers!

I owe you my blackest silence,
my resolve, my indulgence
for all these empty-seeming days,
and whatever is left me of pride
for a blaze in the desert.

But let there be silence
on these lofty figureheads!
The ardent voyage continues,
the course is set on hope.

When will it be your turn, when mine?

The course is set on hope.

1935

MAX

Max,
you are dead
at the age of twenty-three,
dead without having known either peaceful work
or love.

Max,
you were condemned by your youth.
It weighed
on your shoulders like a cross
in the cities and prisons
of Europe.

Your youth condemned you
to the certain death of soldiers
—because the whole human springtime
of this era had to die.
What have they avenged on your proletarian destiny
with prison, with famine,
with the vermin
that gnawed your flesh, your heart
when we were kept
behind barbed wire,
held in sordid jails
by obscure, gloomy,
cowardly, sad, desolate men?

How people died there, brother!
With bitter hearts, hungry bellies,
lice sucking the skin, hate
making its rounds in the brain,
its old rounds,
its exasperating, invigorating old rounds.

But you remained like a child,
purer, better, like a
vaguely triumphant child,
and you loved, in the distance and here,
the great suffering for the great dream,
the great conquest begun
by the murdered communes.

In the sea's salt breeze
hope unfurled in you
all morning and all evening.
That was very good and very bitter.

Then through days of rioting,
through long days of hunger,
through long days of war,
you bore the sadness
and anguish
of your condemned youth.

You suffered from not having found
in the sky of this poor country
the star glimpsed at sea.

(We have yet to conquer it,
we have to make it ourselves
with our hands, with our lives,
with our deaths,
with your death . . .)

The city, with its cold palaces
where the revolution is hungry,
with its gray people in arms,
with those girls on the street,
and all those soldiers departing,
and all those women in tears
in the railroad stations—
the wounded city suffered in you.

And that was your whole life.
And our mutilated victories
were your faith.

Max,
among the sacrificed childhoods
yours was needed.

All the young, broken wings,
all the slaughtered valiant
are necessary to what is being born.

Max,
for the silent rising of the sap
in the branches of young birches,
for the sprouting of the wheat,
for the future glory of ideas,
for this human ascent,
the deaths of thousands of young men
were necessary.

For the victory
of workers republics
come to rebuild the world
on the graves,
your anonymous death,
your foresaken death,
your loveless death,
your forgotten death,
your death, Max,
was no doubt necessary
on that hospital cot,
amid what mortal agonies,
—through what immense shipwreck of everything in you?

Max, it was necessary—
your last look of reproach
and anxious interrogation

toward the living, indifferent ones
at the moment when the last sweat
moistened your poor unhaloed brow.

And you are dead like the others:

Forgive us our surviving you.

Petrograd, 1921

CITY

Ash, granite,
ice, snow, gold
on metal and (crushed)
flesh.

Your cathedrals are icebergs,
your estuary is an ice field.
Cold torments your granite,
and your granite binds a river.

Your river is crystal beneath a meter of snow,
but under this river, in the darkness, another river
carries the secret waters of the North toward the ocean.

Architects designed your least feature,
your vast curves, right angles, colonnades,
a dead city ideal for future tourists.

In your squares, bronze horsemen eternalize
their ancient, despotic gestures
—much prized by filmmakers.

Poets lived gloomily
among your defeated people.

Engineers, despots, and poets—
your people without rights or joy nourished,
glorified,
understood,
betrayed them,
carried them to their graves
in the purest winters
beneath the whitest snows.

City, city, vast city,
vast, immobile city,
I know full well there are flames
devouring you beneath the snow.
In the depths of your open northern skies,
in the depths of the open eyes of your dead,
the steely Pole Star
inscribes its lofty certitude.

City, city, vast city—
golden spires, granite, domes—
sail on, sail on toward the Pole.

Life under granite,
flame under ice.

You are not a cemetery,
you are an immense vessel—
the first one bound
for the dawn or for death.

This is a voyage with no return
—city, city, it's time to set off.

Petrograd, 1920

AUGUST 26, 1928

I ran through the city, I read the papers,
I saw people in offices;
someone lied to me, I lied back,
we smiled,
and I was paid for the unnecessary wear and tear on my brain.

I greeted a dead man. It was raining lightly
on the cheap red wooden coffin.
Some drunks were singing.

You were still living.

One must be strong, one must be hard,
one must go on,
I will go on,
but really, it's hard.

And always we have to understand!

Come into my eyes, tranquility of a summer evening,
I'm in dire need.
—The train stopped, and it was night,
and it was midnight.

Detskoe-Selo, foliage at the windows,
the house asleep,
our breaths mixing,
electric light,
the absurd sorrow that had to be shaken off,
nerves, fatigue, we let ourselves go.

And it was over, some lines written,
it was midnight, it was one o'clock

—I will go on—
the hour of your death.

Brother, comrade, they killed you last night,
at exactly this time.

The transparent night caressed the steppe,
stars rained down on the cornfields.
The enormous black wounds in the sky frightened you.

Kurgannya Road,
Armavir District,
Kuban Region,
red wheat land,
August 26, 1928.

Farewell, everything is ending, the world, brothers, plains,
eyes,
snow, cities, stars,
the International,
farewell, it's insane, why, why,
we are men,
I don't want—

The anguish is immense.
Sawed-off rifle, shapeless bullet,
pierced heart,
split skull, the rifle butt is heavy,
death is light.
Silence.

Brother, your thoughts passed away
through the black wound of the sky.

August 26-30, 1928

THE DEATH OF PANAIT ISTRATI

Finished: the Mediterranean, Paris is finished, finished,
finished that corner of Alexandria where you almost died of hunger,
cholera,
despair
—does anyone know what kills him?

Finished: the romances, dark lips and golden eyes
in the backs of dives, in the ports,
in the depths of the night.

Finished: the bitter and intoxicating temptations
of the sea,
the *Andros* heads toward Piraeus,
the *Santa Mercedes* toward Brindisi, the Indies,
Indonesia,
and you, you stay, eager and sad and penniless on the edge of a
    hotel bed
where dark braids drift across breasts whose moonlight
your hands caress . . .
You quarrel with her and love her, it's stupid, your poem,
    Angelique, Genevieve,
you sweet little whore . . .

Finished: the women, the innocents, the consenters, the repenters,
    the betrayed, the abandoned,
the forgiven,
and the most purely loved! The maids at the Salt Lake Inn
are so desirable . . .

Finished: the paprika dishes and the slightly rough red wine
shared with beggars while swapping tall tales . . .
But maybe they were good men,
maybe they were saints,
your pals

in the little café in Braila
where swaggering toughs
smuggled contraband
under the sign of their "Paradise."

"Not one, you see, not one
would've left the other in the lurch.
They weren't a bunch of writers."

Finished: the books admired
the way a child admires the marvelous
stones
gathered at the seashore,
thrown up from the floor of the sea . . .

Finished: the books written . . .
God! the copies! people who haven't made any don't know
what it's about
and how fed up you can get!

The pages sold, the pages lost, the true, the false,
this pile of big and little lies, all those words
that are traps, junk, trickery—
and the legend!
The sad pages that you are ashamed of having written
and those that you did not know how to extract from your brain . . .
The tiresome, discouraging, exhausting pages
that suddenly come to life
where Nerrantsula struts, more beautiful and proud
and happy to be alive than in real life
—where Nerrantsula walks off, swinging her hips,
and dives into the Danube under the open sky,
O white swimmer, in love with the water . . .
The heart of hearts of men that you spit out in your work.
Can Reider's still be selling all that printed paper?

Finished: the insults.
They did not stint there.

They got fat on stuffing them down your throat until your death
    and even after.
So
thanks to you many people ate better than you.
They said that you were a traitor, that you sold out, my poor friend!
To think of you, the faithful one, betraying all those phrase-
    mongers,
you, a sellout, who never had anything to sell, and yourself
    unsalable!
You lay upon your press clippings, like Job upon his ashes,
quietly spitting the last bit of your lungs
in the faces of those copy-pissers,
glorifiers of profitable massacres,
profiteers of disfigured revolutions . . .

Finished: even the wish to die
when only bastards are left in this vale of promotional tears.
For you botched it earlier because you loved the earth too much.
It left you with a scar across the carotid
and your suicide attempt made it hard to wear false collars.

Your last unfinished pages leave you
like a flight of doves,
darkness and ash, return to darkness, return to ash—
you would like to cry, but that's not possible, oh sure,
cry, you must be joking!

You stumble, the road's burning stones slip from under your feet,
"Hold me up, my pretty friends!" Hold him, friends, hold him,
the sky is so blinding, it's heartbreaking!
You go off between two goddesses, they reassure you, they carry you
    away,
consoling you:
solitude, friendship.

Never again will I see you pass from room to room
in a black mood
with your cup of black coffee.

Never again will I calm your wild rages.
Never again will I see your veined Balkan hands,
your big, gold-filled mouth,
your hunter's nose, your sly child's eyes,
a cynic among the cunning . . .
And we will not go to Provence with packs on our backs to take
    pictures as if we were twenty,
no charge for the most beautiful girl and the madman, the
    betrothed and the anarchist . . .
Those were good times.

Nights, I've sighed over you so often
that this evening, in this desert, I feel closer to you than to the
    living.
The same winds blow across my steppe and your Baragan,
the same storms . . .
The Big Dipper sparkles in my window;
and behind the house stretches the plain, so vast
and naked that it seems like the edge of the earth.
A young woman is sleeping here in the fatigue of her work
and the calm of her giving.

The fresh sadness of your death torments and soothes me.
All this is your tomb and it will be mine and is already ours,
our continued life.

I am listening in your stead,
what radiant silence falls on the clamor.

Orenburg, 1935

WHY INSCRIBE A NAME?

In the Kok Tebel cemetery in the Blue Mountains,
the Tartars put only a stone on their graves,
not even cut, without inscription.

Why inscribe a name when the man is no more?
For us? Do you actually believe, they ask, that we could ever forget
    him?
For God? But God knows him for all eternity.

These wise men are thus unaware of the administration
and its profitable traffic in thirty-year concessions
and the bourgeois pleasure of buying oneself a monumental vault
more expensive
than the fate of a poor man
        or the house of a proletarian.

CASSIOPEIA

You told me, Oxana, that he died this morning
despite you,
despite your youth, despite your prettiness, your pity, your hands,
your care,
you told me of your anguish over the death of this unknown man,
without name, age, or face,
resembling from a distance the crucified Christ, but more naked,
he who had been drinking his cup in little sips for years between
    temperature charts and banishment orders.
"Oh, if only I could have tried those last injections," you were
    saying.
"But I wasn't on duty until eleven o'clock,
his heart had already failed,
I only found him at the morgue, with his pure features."

The names of diseases, Oxana, are words
that we throw at the ills, the wounds, the deaths at work within us.
The heart, that old, relentless, excitable, and cunning organ, is
    abused.
What could your little vials and aseptic needles do
when the whole planet is falling apart from exhaustion?

Tracked down, this dead man I never saw is right here,
now that he no longer exists, he has followed us through this
    holiday.
And when I put my hand on Tatiana's shoulder, the Other who is in
    me, who is bigger and better than me, who knows the secret,
    said to the dead man close by:
"This hand is yours and I give you this shoulder.
Young woman, you must give him your shoulder—let him lean on
    it—you must give him everything, you understand: he's dead,
he now has nothing but our warmth, he has only my arms to
    embrace you,

and no one in the world but you, since I am the only one who
    knows."

The bands have gone by, and the slightly grotesque tanks,
the flags, the processions, the soldiers
singing of the towns taken on the shores of the Pacific,
the athletes have gone by, and the blue clouds that caressed the
    steppe.
There was a little barefoot Mongol shepherd wearing a felt hat who
    jauntily followed the snapping flags, like a singer of paeans,
he's gone now—
you remain.

The day, with its noise and the brilliance of sun and brass, is over;
alone with you, I have this granted shoulder, this naked breast, this
    consenting mouth, this forgiven soul, close to me, close to you,
and all your departed warmth is in me.

Dear, unknown dead man, haven't I misjudged, disdained, insulted
    you in our separate lives,
our crippled lives,
now,
you, frozen underground, we, standing on the earth, nothing
    separates us anymore, reunited as we are by the risen stars and
    this sign between us: the high glittering triangles of Cassiopeia.

Orenburg, summer 1935

SONG

Destins, destins impénétrables . . .
—Apollinaire

Destinies impenetrable destinies
cities are built on sand
but the deserts will bloom again
O heart of the inexhaustible world
hope refuses to die

this hard will my dear madness
suffer, suffer, you must smile
whether the wound bleeds or cries
the gods have nothing more to say to you
the jungle is your only home

the earth has the eyes of panthers
do you really love the earth
sky ripped by comets
absurd child in despair
are you the victim of poets

archer who watches and forgives
O you who never give up
welcome this shadow born for you
doesn't it give all its pride
to every passerby come from you

the archer succumbs the stone splits
the flower is a triumphant cry
do you want us to be brothers
I bring a light into the void
nothing will obscure this radiance

Imagine if you found peace again

what sea spreads out beneath the palms
the flesh requires the knife
did you betray the dawn of peace
night devours the torches

for me a single blaze remains
I am standing, nothing more will die
totter O Cordillera of the Andes
the fervor of Elbrus' pure snows
unite your ardent heights

divine spinning planet
your Eurasias your singing seas
the simple scorn of executioners
and here we have merciful thoughts
almost like heros.

TRUST

I've seen the steppe turn green and the child grow;
my eyes meet the human gaze
of my good old dog Toby, who trusts me.

The azure touches the earth, we breathe in the sky.
Red cows graze under clouds of glory,
and from afar the slim Kirgiz woman who tends them
seems released from all misery.

Setting sun, here are our breasts, take them!
Here are our bodies that you fill with radiance,
here we are washed,
purified,
liberated,
pacified,
at the point where river, plain, and sky touch.

Nothing is forgotten, nothing is lost, we are faithful,
faithfully men, men faithful to men
regardless of the moment, the risk, the burden, the pain,
the hate,
faithful and trusting.

My son, my tall son, we are going to cleave the water
with slow strokes—
let's trust in the river pierced by sunbeams,
trust in these waters drunk by our brothers, the drowned.

Trust in the frail, supple muscles of the child
who dives from the steep bank and then cries out:
"O father, it's terrible and good, I'm touching bottom,
the light is mixed with darkness and it's quivering, quivering . . . "

Grace of the slender body darting through the air, through the
     water,
trust with eyes closed, trust with eyes open.

What could be more parabolic than this flight of birds?
My mind follows it, just as lively, just as sure,
an arrow through abstract space,
laden with moving images by all that was,
ethereal and prodigal,
offering the future many possible futures.

The scarab sleeps on the wild rose,
our shadows scared off the tadpoles in the pond,
a magnificent, peaceful day and the earth goes on
carrying off days, nights, dawns, evenings,
tropics, poles, deserts,
cities,
and our thoughts,
our common journey through the infinite,
the eternal,
the eyes,
toward the constellation of Hercules, itself swept along
by such great floods of stars that all night fades
—defeat swept away . . .

Orenburg, 1934

SENSATION
for L. "Don't be sad . . ."

After that splendid Notre Dame inverted
in a Seine free of the vagrants' remorse,
after that trembling rose window blooming in the black water
where the stars spin out their inconceivable threads
through profiles of sea horses and foliage as real
as mirages,

what is left, O my insanely reasonable spirit,

what remains inaccessible to the awakened sleeper
who follows down these dark quays,
from one Commune to the next,
the hopeful cortege of his executed brothers?

Paris, 1938

Мэхико 1947. Swernavoe 1948

А.Р.

HANDS

Terra-cotta by a 16th-century Italian artist, sometimes attributed to Michelangelo.
London Museum.

What astonishing contact, old man, your hands establish with our
   own!
How vain the centuries of death before your hands . . .

The artist, nameless like you, surprised them in the act of grasping
—who knows if the gesture still vibrates or has just ended?
The veins pulse, they are old veins toughened by the song of the
   blood,
Oh, what are they grasping, your hands of fading strength,
do they cling to earth, do they cling to flesh
for the last or the next-to-last time,
are they gathering the crystal containing purity,
are they caressing the living darkness containing fertility,
are they patient,
are they determined, ardent, resistant,
are they secretly weak?
What is certain is their pride.

The veins of your hands, old man, express prayer,
the prayer of your blood, old man, the next-to-last
prayer,
neither verbal prayer nor clerical prayer,
but the prayer of conscious ardor,
potent—impotent.
Their presence confronts the world with itself,
questions it as one questions what one loves
definitively

57

without any possible response.

Am I alone, I deaf, I so separated from you,
I so detached from myself,
Am I as alone in knowing as you are,
I alone at this moment and reaching out to you
through time?

Or are we alone together
among all those who in the course of time are alone with us,
forming the one choir that murmurs in our shared veins,
our singing veins?

I wanted to tell you, old man, something moving,
moved,
fraternal,
to find for you, in the name of all others, a naked word
in the northern lights
in the glow on the glaciers,
a simple, intimate, and loyal word.

You, you didn't know
that the veins in the temples of the electrocuted
boil like knots of rebellious blood
under the skin glistening with sweat more horrible than the sweat of
    Christ on the cross.
Someone told me the sight recalled
a fly stalked by a strange spider,
and the fly a soul that had been saved.

Oh, what could I do, oh what could I do to soothe your veins,
I who know torture, you who know torture,
we must yet be capable, for each other,
from one end of time to the other,
of throwing into the inexorable balance of the universe
at least the fragility of a thought, a sign, a line of verse
that perhaps has neither substance nor radiance yet exists,
as real as the imploring veins of your hand,

as real as my veins, so little different . . .

May the final glow of the final dawn,
may the final intermittent star,
may the final distress in the final waiting,
may the final smile of the serene mask
be on the veins of your hand, old man I've found.

A drop of blood falls from one sky to another,
dazzling.

Our hands are unconscious, tough, ascendant, conscious,
plainsong, delighted suffering,
nailed to rainbows.
Together, together, joined,
they have here seized
the unexpected.

And we didn't know
that together we held
this dazzling thing.

A drop of blood—
a single ray of light falls from one hand to the other,
dazzling.

Mexico, November 1947

CITY LIGHTS PUBLICATIONS

Mrabet, Mohammed. LOVE WITH A FEW HAIRS
Mrabet, Mohammed. M'HASHISH
Murguia, Alejandro, ed. VOLCAN: Poems from Central America
O'Hara, Frank. LUNCH POEMS
Olson, Charles. CALL ME ISHMAEL
Orlovsky, Peter. CLEAN A POEMS
Paschke, Barbara, ed. CLAMOR OF INNOCENCE: Stories
    from Central America
Pessoa, Fernando. ALWAYS ASTONISHED: Selected Prose
Pasolini, Pier Paolo. ROMAN POEMS
Poe, Edgar Alan. THE UNKNOWN POE
Porta, Antonio. KISSES FROM ANOTHER DREAM
Purdy, James. GARMENTS THE LIVING WEAR
Purdy, James. IN A SHALLOW GRAVE
Prévert, Jacques. PAROLES
Rey-Rosa, Rodrigo. THE BEGGAR'S KNIFE
Rigaud, Milo. SECRETS OF VOODOO
Saadawi El, Nawal. MEMOIRS OF A WOMAN DOCTOR
Sawyer-Lauçanno, Christopher, transl. THE DESTRUCTION OF THE
    JAGUAR: Poems from the Books of Chilam Balam
Sclauzero, Mariarosa. MARLENE
Serge, Victor. RESISTANCE
Shepard, Sam. MOTEL CHRONICLES
Shepard, Sam. FOOL FOR LOVE & THE SAD LAMENT
    OF PECOS BILL
Smith, Michael. IT A COME
Snyder, Gary. THE OLD WAYS
Tutuola, Amos. FEATHER WOMAN OF THE JUNGLE
Tutuola, Amos. SIMBI & THE SATYR OF THE DARK JUNGLE
Waley, Arthur. THE NINE SONGS
Wilson, Colin. POETRY AND MYSTICISM